Fashion Design

by Tiffany Peterson

illustrations by David Westerfield

Heinemann Library
Chicago, Illinois

©2003 Heinemann Library
a division of Reed Elsevier Inc.
Chicago, Illinois

Customer Service 888-454-2279
Visit our website at www.heinemannlibrary.com

Designed by Depke Design
Illustrated by David Westerfield
Photograph p. 4 by Kimberly Saar
Printed and bound in the United States by Lake Book Manufacturing, Inc.
07 06 05 04 03
10 9 8 7 6 5 4 3 2 1

Library of Congress Cataloging-in-Publication Data
Peterson, Tiffany.
  Fashion designs / Tiffany Peterson; illustrations by David Westerfield.
    p. cm. -- (Draw it!)

  Summary: Presents instructions for drawing an outfit from each decade of the twentieth century, as well as a colonial open robe dress and a design of one's own. Includes bibliographical references and index.
  ISBN 1-4034-0211-6 (HC), 1-4034-4030-1 (Pbk)
  1. Fashion drawing--Juvenile literature. [1. Fashion drawing. 2. Drawing--Technique.] I. Westerfield, David, 1956- ill. II. Title. III. Series.
  TT509.P48 2003
  741.6'72--dc21
                                 2002015489

Some words are shown in bold, **like this.** You can find out what they mean by looking in the glossary.

Contents

Introduction

Would you like to improve the pictures that you draw?

Well, you can! In this book, the artist has drawn some different fashions. He has used lines and shapes to draw each picture in small, simple steps. Follow these steps and your picture will come together for you, too.

Here is advice from the artist:

- Always draw lightly at first.

- Draw all the shapes and pieces in the right places.

- Pay attention to the spaces between the lines as well as the lines themselves.

- Add details and **shading** to finish your drawing.

- And finally, erase the lines you don't need.

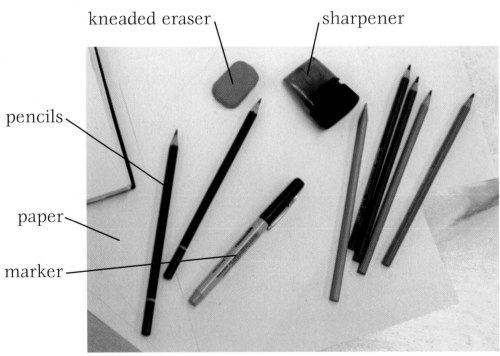

You only need a few supplies to get started.

There are just four things you need for drawing:

- a pencil (medium or soft). You might also use a fine marker or pen to finish your drawing.
- a pencil sharpener.
- paper.
- an eraser. A **kneaded eraser** works best. It can be squeezed into small or odd shapes. This eraser can also make the pencil lines lighter without erasing them.

Now, are you ready? Do you have everything?
Then turn the page and let's draw!

The drawings in this book were done by David Westerfield. David started drawing when he was very young. In college, he studied drawing and painting. Now he is a **commercial artist** who owns his own graphic design business. He has two children, and he likes to draw with them. David's advice to anyone who hopes to become an artist is to "practice, practice, practice–and learn as much as you can from other artists."

Draw an American Colonial Dress

The style of this dress is called open robe. The dress is like a robe worn over a full skirt. The top of the robe is kept closed by a piece of fabric called a stomacher. Stomachers have hooks on each side that connect to the inside of the robe. During the 1700s, stomachers were often decorated with bows or ruffles.

1 Start by **sketching** a big bell shape for the skirt. Draw a smaller bell shape that is upside down for the **bodice.** These are your **guidelines.**

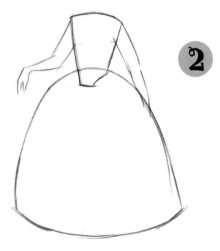

2 Sketch one arm by drawing a shape like a banana connected to the shoulder. Draw two **vertical** lines for the hand. Add a small curved line for the curved finger. The other arm is straight. Draw two **parallel** lines from the shoulder to a point about one third down on the skirt.

3 Add an egg shape for the head. Connect it to the body by drawing two short, slightly curved lines for the neck. Add guidelines for the eyes, nose, and mouth.

4 Draw two short curved lines for the eyebrows. Below the eyebrows, draw two more short lines for her eyes. Draw a slightly curved L shape for the nose. Add a line for the mouth. Draw a curved line above one eye for the hairline. Draw a half circle on top of the head for a **bun** and a very small curved line for the ear. Add some curvy lines at the elbows for the ruffles of her sleeves.

5 Draw two lines from the shoulders and connect them with a wavy line for a neckline. Add ruffles to the sides of the neckline. Draw a line along each side of the bodice so they almost meet at the bottom and form an open V. Draw wavy lines in the V for ruffles in the bodice. In the skirt, draw two lines from the bodice to the **hem** that are parallel to the outline. Draw lines inside the skirt to show the fabric folds. Draw a small rounded square at the hem for a foot.

6 Erase the guidelines you no longer need. Add the last details. The necklace is a half circle around the neck with an oval at the bottom. Add the lower lip by drawing a short line parallel to the line you drew for the mouth. Darken the lines and add **shading** along the folds.

Draw a Civil War Dress

Like the American colonial open robe dress, this fashion of the Civil War period has a full skirt. In 1856, the "cage" **crinoline** was invented. It was a series of steel hoops connected with strips of fabric and worn under the dress.

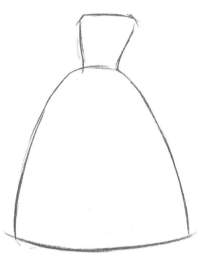

1 Draw a bell shape for the skirt. Add a smaller, upside down bell shape on top for the **bodice.** Where these two shapes meet is the waistline.

2 Add the arms. Draw a slanted V for the left elbow. Draw a **vertical** line to finish the shape of the forearm. Sketch the rough shape of a hand as if the woman were pointing to herself. Draw two curved **parallel** lines from the other shoulder. Add two vertical lines for the forearm. Draw half of an oval for the shape of the hand.

3 Draw an oval for the head. Add two short vertical lines for the neck and short angled lines for the shoulders. Add **guidelines** for the eyes, nose, and mouth.

4 Sketch a wavy line for the ruffle on the right sleeve. Add two parallel lines around her wrists for wristbands. Add fingers to the hands. Draw a diamond shape with notches in the bottom edge for a handkerchief in the right hand. Add a wiggly line for the neckline. Add the eyebrows, eyes, and nose. Draw a line for the mouth and a short line under it. Draw the hair with short curvy lines.

5 Sketch several wavy lines across the skirt. Draw a wavy line along the bottom, or **hem,** of the skirt. Draw a V shape at the waistline. Add short vertical lines from the waistline and between the skirt's wavy lines to show folds. Add a wavy line below the neckline from one arm to the middle of the bodice. Sketch small wavy ovals at the middle of the wavy line and on the right shoulder for flower **ornaments.**

6 Darken all of the lines on the skirt. Add vertical lines to the skirt to make it look ruffled. Shade in the top of the hair. Add shading around the bottom of the skirt for the ground.

Draw a Suffragette

At the beginning of the 1900s, women were fighting for the right to vote. As women tried to get the rights and freedoms that men had, women's fashions became more relaxed. In fact, women of this period stopped using **corsets**. Corsets had been used for many years to make women's waists tiny enough to fit in high-fashion dresses. A woman did not need a tiny waist to wear the dress style shown here.

1 **Sketch** a square that is smaller on the bottom than the top for the bodice. Under the square, sketch a bell shape for the skirt. The line between the **bodice** and the skirt is the waistline.

2 Sketch two sideways Vs for the left arm. For the right arm, draw one curved line from the top of the bodice. Add another curved line from the waistline. Sketch two sets of two **vertical** lines from the bottom of the skirt for ankles. Add curved lines for feet, with the tips of triangles for the toes. Add slight curves for heels.

3 Draw an oval for the head. Draw **guidelines** for the eyes, nose, and mouth. Add two curved lines from the neck to the shoulders and two straight lines to the collar area.

4 Draw small lines for eyebrows, eyes, nose, and the mouth. Sketch an oval around the top of the head for the **brim** of the hat. Add the top of the hat. Sketch a flower shape on the hat for an **ornament.** Draw two lines above each wrist for the sleeve cuffs. Add the hands and fingers.

5 Draw a V with a horizontal line under it for the neckline. Add two triangles for the **lapels.** Draw two vertical lines each from both the left shoulder and the right shoulder to the waistline. Add a horizontal line across the waistline for the belt. Sketch a rectangle over each of the left and right sides of the skirt for the bottom parts of the coat. Draw zigzag lines at the bottom of the rectangles. Draw two long rectangles along the inside edges of the coat. Draw a zigzag line along the bottom of the skirt. Add the puffy lines of the shapes around the arms.

6 Erase the guidelines you no longer need. Darken the rest of the lines. Sketch a long V with a circle at the bottom for a necklace. Add **shading** in the coat and under the chin. Draw a long thin loop on the front of the shoes for decoration. Add some shading around the feet.

Draw a 1920s Flapper

In the 1920s, skirts and dresses became shorter as hemlines went up. During this time period, women tried to look boyish. They often "bobbed" their hair, cutting it in a short style. The dresses had straight lines. Waistlines were out, but showing a lot of leg was in.

1 **Sketch** two wavy lines. Connect them at the top with a line that curves up for a shoulder line. Connect them at the bottom with a **horizontal** line. Draw two **parallel** horizontal lines, like a belt, that are higher on the left side than on the right. These lines show the waistline.

2 Sketch two sideways Vs for the bent arm. Sketch the hand by drawing two lines above the waistline. The other arm is hidden, but the hand rests at the hip. Sketch the hand by drawing a long triangle with a V in it for the thumb.

3 Draw two parallel **vertical** lines for the neck from the middle of the shoulder line. Add a long oval for the head. Lightly sketch a horizontal line in the oval as a **guideline** for the eyes.

4 For the right leg, sketch two vertical lines that slightly curve and come to a point at the bottom. Draw one long line and one shorter line for the left leg. To draw the sideways left shoe, draw a short curved line from the bottom of the short leg line. Draw a short horizontal line for the shoe bottom. Add an upside down V to make the heel.

5 Sketch a large V for the neckline. To put a bow above the left hand, draw a circle for the knot. Add two rectangles, a small one and a large one, for the bow. Draw three wavy lines across the skirt. Add shading near the chest.

6 Sketch a pointy oval for the top of the hair. Draw two curved lines from the left top of her hair to just above the jaw for a curl. Color in the hair. Draw an earring under the curl. Add eyebrows, eyes, nose, and mouth. Add a long half oval for a necklace. Draw several vertical lines down the skirt for fringe. Darken all lines. Add some **shading** on the sides of the skirt, around the armhole and above the waistline. Draw a curved line across the toes for shoes.

 Draw a 1930s Day Dress

Hemlines went down again in the 1930s, but not like they had been in the 1800s. Dresses of the 1930s were more elegant than the boyish straight-lined dresses of the 1920s. Dress lines were simple and showed off the shape of a woman's body. These simple lines did not include pockets, so the handbag became an important accessory.

1 **Sketch** a long shape like a curvy tube for the skirt. Add an upside down bell shape for the **bodice.** The line where the two shapes come together is the waistline. Add a curved line across the waistline. This is the belt.

2 Sketch two sideways Vs for the left arm. Draw two slightly bent **parallel** lines from the right shoulder for the right arm. Draw a shape like a snake's head for the left leg. Draw a parallel line to the right of that leg. Curve the line to the left at the end. Draw a triangle on the other side of the left leg for the toes of the right foot.

3 Add two curved lines for the neck. Sketch an egg shape as a **guideline** for the head. Draw a curved line across the middle of the head. Add a triangle shape to finish the hat's **brim.**

4 Draw a small turned L for the nose and a small sideways V for the mouth. Add three curved lines at the back of the head for hair. Draw a small circle under these lines for the **bun.** Draw a half circle for the neckline. Draw two small curved lines at the bottom of the neck. Sketch the gloves. The top of each glove looks like the top of a heart. Add lines for the fingers. Draw a curved line across the toes for shoes.

5 Add several **vertical** lines inside the belt for the buckle. Add a wavy line below the belt for the bottom of the jacket. Draw wavy lines on the arms for the edges of the short sleeves. Add two shapes like the bottom of a man's necktie along the neckline. Draw a half circle under the neckline. Sketch lines inside the skirt, the bodice, and the sleeves to show folds in the fabric. Add a wavy line on the **hem.**

6 Erase the guidelines that you don't need. Add a band around the hat by drawing two curved lines. **Shade** the band and add two triangle shapes for a bow at the back of the hat. Add a curved rectangle for the purse. Color in the purse. Draw several dark curvy lines, like pleats, along the right side of the skirt. Shade the skirt, the arms, and the bodice. Add several vertical lines along the bottom of the skirt. Shade the back of the neck. Add shading for the ground.

Draw a 1940s WAC

During World War II, the Army asked women to join the Women's Army Corps (WAC) and serve in military hospitals and offices. A lot of planning went into the uniform. The jacket looked like the men's military uniform. However, many women thought it was not right to wear shorts or pants, so the WACs replaced pants with knee-length skirts.

1 Draw an upside down bell shape with a curved bottom. Add a long **vertical** line on the right and a long curved line on the left. Connect the two lines with a **horizontal** line at the bottom for a skirt. Add a curved line across the middle for the waistline.

2 **Sketch** two sideways Vs for the left arm and two for the right arm. Add the shape of the curved right hand. Draw a line curving down from the right bottom of the skirt for a leg. Add a curved line for the inside of the leg and heel of the shoe. Add the bottom of the shoe. Draw two slightly curved lines for the left leg. Make the left line slightly curve out. Connect the two lines with a curve.

3 Add two short vertical lines for the neck and an oval for the head. Lightly sketch **guidelines** for the eyes, nose, and mouth.

4 Sketch a square on top of the head for the hat. Add a point to the middle of the square's bottom line. Draw a wavy line for the top of the hat. Add curly hair by drawing wavy lines around the face. Add the eyebrows, eyes, nose, and mouth. Draw a small V close to the neck for the neckline. Sketch a wavy line for the left hand's knuckles just outside the skirt's line. Draw a square with a line across it for the handbag. Draw two **parallel** lines across the wrists for the jacket cuffs. Draw the tips of the fingers. Draw two lines across the left shoe and a line across the right foot.

5 Draw two sideways Ms on either side of the neck for the **lapels.** Add an X for the tie. Draw an upside down V at the top of the X to connect the lines. Draw a wavy line from the lapels to the waistline. Add two square pockets to the jacket. Add a curved line to the waistline for the belt. Draw folds on the sleeves. Draw two long lines from the shoulder to the belt, and two short lines from the back corner of the bag to the arm for the bag straps. Add an oval and a circle for the **clasp** of the bag. Draw a **vertical** line down the middle of the skirt.

6 Erase guidelines that you don't need and darken the rest. Color the hair. Add a square on the hat with a vertical line through the center for **bars.** Add two vertical lines to the pockets and draw buttons. Add a pocket on the right arm. Color the purse, leaving parts of it white so it looks glossy. **Shade** the skirt. Color the shoes, jacket, and hat. Add shading to the left sides of the legs.

Draw a 1950s Dior

Christian Dior created a style called the New Look. Dior dresses had broad shoulders, a small waist, and full hips. Women again wore layered **petticoats** to create full skirts. Luckily, in the 1950s petticoats were no longer made of heavy cotton. They were made of light netting.

1 **Sketch** a bell shape for the skirt. Be sure to leave room for the legs and feet underneath. Draw a smaller upside down bell shape for the **bodice.** Darken the line between the skirt and the bodice to show the waistline.

2 Add the right arm by drawing two **parallel** lines from the right shoulder. Sketch the hand by adding two curved lines from the bottom of the arm. Draw two more lines from the left shoulder. Add a round shape for the hand. Draw one straight leg from the center of the skirt. Add several curved lines as a **guideline** for a high-heeled shoe. Draw the second leg and shoe at an angle.

3 Draw two curved lines for the neck. Add a pointed oval for the head. Draw dashes for guidelines for the mouth, nose and eyes.

4 Draw the nose, mouth, eyebrow, and eye. Sketch the hair by drawing a wavy line from the forehead to the top of the neck. Finish the hair by drawing a curved line from the neck to the back of the head. Sketch the hat. Draw half of an oval starting at the top of the forehead. Continue drawing from the half oval as if drawing an upside down slipper. Draw curved lines across the elbows of the arms for the tops of the gloves. Sketch the fingers. Add curved lines above the toes for the shoes.

5 Make the armholes of the sleeveless dress by drawing curved lines from the tops of the shoulders to the sides of the bodice. Draw a wide V for the neckline. Continue the left side of the V to the waistline. Add a **sash** by drawing two curved parallel lines at the waistline. Draw several dark **vertical** lines from the sash for folds. Sketch several lines at the edges of the skirt.

6 Erase the guidelines that you don't need. Draw several **horizontal** lines along the gloves for folds. **Shade** the gloves and the hat. Add a dark **veil** at the front of the hat. Shade the bodice and skirt of the dress to show folds. Shade the ground and then the neck under the chin and the tops of the legs for shadow.

Draw a 1960s Minidress

1960s youth **rebelled** against the styles of the 1950s. Women's hair styles got shorter, and so did the dresses. Dresses in the 1960s became so short, in fact, they were called mini dresses. Clothes in the 1960s were often made with bright colors and bold patterns.

1 **Sketch** a rectangle with curvy sides.

2 Sketch two backwards 7s for the left arm. Sketch a long, thin rectangle for the right leg. Add the rough shape of the foot at the bottom by drawing a line that angles out. Draw another rectangle at an angle for the left leg. Add the foot by drawing two lines that angle out.

3 Sketch a pointed oval for the head. Add two lines for the neck. Add a curl at the back of the jaw line for the ear. At the bottom of the neck on the right, draw a short, slanted line. Sketch two **horizontal** lines as **guidelines** for the eyes and nose.

4 Draw several lines for the hair along the forehead. Draw the eyebrow, eye, nose, and mouth. Draw a circle for a large hoop earring. Add the hand and three fingers. The fourth finger and the thumb are hidden. Draw a line across each leg just below the knee for the tops of the boots. Sketch in short lines for knees. Darken the lines for the boots and add a heel to the right boot with a small rectangle.

5 Sketch a curved line for the neckline and part of an oval for the left armhole. Draw a line from near the bottom of the armhole across the dress. Add a short curved line above this for the right shoulder. Sketch a short curved line along the edge at the middle of the right side for the right arm. Sketch a shape like a stop sign on the dress near the hand. Draw lines coming out from each corner of the stop sign shape.

6 Erase the guidelines that you do not need. Darken the lines in the picture. **Shade** in the hair. Color in the dress. Add some shading around the feet for the ground. Shade the legs so they look different from the boots.

Draw a 1970s Pantsuit

Women had been wearing pants for decades. In the 1970s, pants and pantsuits could be worn to dressy and formal events for the first time. The shoes in this drawing are called platform shoes. They were very popular in the 1970s.

1 **Sketch** two ovals.

2 Connect the circles with two curved lines. Add a slightly pointed oval for the head. Sketch three **horizontal** lines as **guidelines** for the eyes, nose, and mouth. Add two short curved lines for the neck.

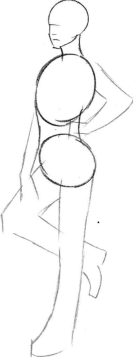

3 Draw a sideways V for the right arm. Add slightly bent vertical lines for the left arm. Draw two long **vertical** lines for the right leg. Make the left line curve out at the end. Sketch a rectangle for the foot. Draw two sideways Vs for the left leg. Sketch half of a slanted rectangle for the toe of the shoe. Add a line for the back of the heel.

4 Draw two Vs for the collar. Sketch two curved lines across the waist for the belt. Add a small square for the belt buckle. Add a line from the collar to the waist and short curvy lines around the left arm for the sleeve. Draw a line across the upper part of the right leg and an upside down V for the bottom of the jacket. Draw a curved line across the top of the right shoe for the pant cuff. Add a curved line from the toe area to the cuff on both shoes. Sketch a small rectangle for the heels.

5 Draw a curved line along the top and back of the head. Add jagged lines along the forehead and side of the face for hair. Make a V below the chin on the right to outline the neck. Draw a small sideways V under the chin on the left for hair. Add eyes, eyebrows, mouth, and a curved L shape for the nose. Draw a rectangle slanted up on the right for the right hand and wrist. Draw the left hand with little Us and Vs for fingers.

6 Erase guidelines that you do not need. Draw two lines across each wrist for the sleeve cuffs. Add curvy lines along the edges of the sleeves and legs to show folds in the fabric. Color the hair. Darken the lines of the drawing. **Shade** the ground around her feet.

Draw a 1980s Mini-Crini

In the 1980s, the "mini-crini" appeared. It was a shorter version of the **crinolined** dresses that were popular in the 1950s. The designer added two puffs at the hips to make the woman's hips look wider and her waist smaller.

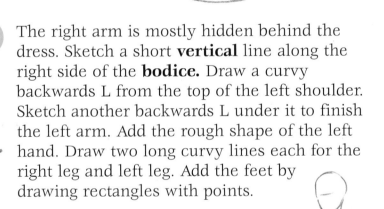

1 Draw a bell shape with a curved rectangle on top of it This is the **guideline** for the dress.

2 The right arm is mostly hidden behind the dress. Sketch a short **vertical** line along the right side of the **bodice.** Draw a curvy backwards L from the top of the left shoulder. Sketch another backwards L under it to finish the left arm. Add the rough shape of the left hand. Draw two long curvy lines each for the right leg and left leg. Add the feet by drawing rectangles with points.

3 Sketch a pointed oval for the head. Draw a short guideline for the eyes. Draw a short line on the left and a longer curved line on the right for the neck.

4 Sketch the hair. Draw a rough triangle on top of the head with a curl coming off the right tip. On both sides of the face, add some wiggly lines for curls and wave. Draw eyebrows, eyes, nose, and mouth. Put a small line on the cheek for a cheekbone. Sketch a curvy line along the top of the original guidelines for the collarbone. Add fingers by drawing tiny V's. Add short lines for knees.

5 Add an upside down V across each of the feet for the tops of the shoes. For the puffs at the waist sketch a sideways 8 with straight lines. Draw a wide M for the top of the dress and a curvy line from the middle point of the M all the way down to the bottom of the dress. Add some lines along the sides of the bodice to show folds in the fabric.

6 Darken all of the lines. Add **shading** to the right arm, the top half of the left arm, and on the tops of the legs. Darken the shading in the dress.

Draw a 1990s Formal Gown

In the 1990s fashion designers looked to the past for ideas. Styles from the 50s, 60s, and 70s came back. Women had many choices in the 1990s. Everything from the mini dress to the full-length gown was stylish. This full-length dress borrows from the fashions of the 1970s.

1 **Sketch** the skirt by drawing a long triangle with no top point. Add an upside down bell shape on top for the **bodice.** The line where these two shapes meet is the waistline.

2 Draw a long **vertical** line from the right shoulder down to the skirt. Add a shorter **parallel** line to finish the **guideline** for the right arm. Draw a tipped L shape starting at the left shoulder. Add a smaller L shape for the rest of the left arm.

3 Sketch a slightly pointed oval for the head. Connect it to the body by drawing two slightly curved lines for the neck. Add lines from the neck to the shoulders. Sketch two **horizontal** lines as guidelines for the eyes and mouth.

4 Draw the nose, mouth, and eye. Add a curved line for the eyebrow. Draw a backwards C for an ear and a tiny circle for an earring. Sketch several horizontal lines from the forehead toward the back of the head for the hair. Add curly hair in the back by drawing two ovals with lines in them at the back of the head. Draw four curved fingers at the waist. Draw a horizontal line across the right wrist for the bottom of the sleeve.

5 Sketch a half of a square with rounded corners for the dress's neckline. Draw a wavy line across the waist. Draw five more wavy lines across the skirt to create a pattern of wide cloud-like stripes. Sketch several vertical lines in the bottom half of the skirt for folds in the fabric. Add a curvy line at the bottom of the skirt for the hemline.

6 Erase the guidelines that you do not need. Darken all of the lines. Add **shading** at the back of the neck and under the chin. Color in the bodice and sleeves of the dress. Add several horizontal lines on the upper half of the left arm for folds. Color in the stripes in the skirt. Add some shading for the ground.

Create Your Own Fashion Design

You can sketch this figure, or human shape, and add clothes to it. Look back through the designs in this book for ideas or create something completely new. Use your imagination and have fun!

1 **Sketch** a large oval. Sketch a smaller **horizontal** oval under it.

2 Sketch a small oval for the head. Add a curved L shape for the face and chin. Draw a **vertical** line at the end of the L shape for the jawline. Add two vertical lines for the neck. Lightly sketch three horizontal lines for **guidelines** for the eyes, nose, and mouth.

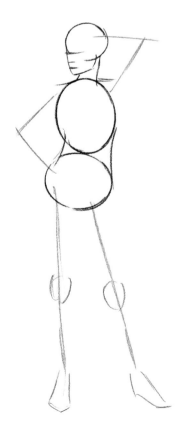

3 Draw a sideways V from each shoulder, one up to the head, the other down to the waist. Draw two long lines for the legs. Add circles for knees. Sketch a triangle shape for the right foot and a long oval for the left foot.

4 Sketch the shape of the body by drawing lines connecting the guideline circles. Draw a line across the shoulders.

5 Draw the shape of the hand on the hip. Add the rough shape of fingers. Shape the ankles and feet. Add a curvy line along the bottom of the right foot.

6 Add hair by drawing a curved line along the back of the head and a bunch of short curved lines along the forehead. Draw curved lines for eyebrows and small dots for eyes. Draw a curved L shape for the nose. Draw two curved lines for the mouth. Add a half circle for the ear. Now add your own fashion design. Sketch the clothes lightly first. Then erase the guidelines that you do not need and darken the lines of the final drawing.

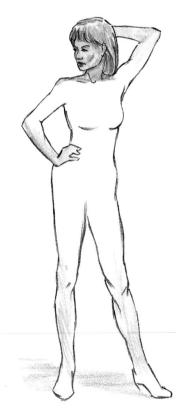

Glossary

accessory extra piece of clothing such as gloves or a handbag worn with an outfit

bars in a military uniform, bars made of metal show the rank, or position, of the person wearing them

bodice top half of a dress

bridge vertical line of the nose

brim edge of a hat that sticks out

bun hairstyle in which all of the hair is pulled back to the top or back of the head and rolled in a ball shape

clasp part of handbag that keeps it closed

corset piece of clothing worn under a dress to make a woman's waist look smaller

crinoline stiff underskirt to make a dress look fuller

hem bottom edge of a skirt or dress

lapels two parts of a jacket or shirt that fold back under the neckline

ornament something that is added to decorate

petticoat full, often ruffled, underskirt worn to make a dress look fuller

rebel to go against

sash wide belt or scarf worn around the waist

veil a piece of see-through fabric that covers the face

Art Glossary

broad line that is fat or wide	**guideline** light line, used to shape a drawing, that is usually erased in the final drawing
horizontal line that is level or flat	**kneaded eraser** soft, squeezable eraser, used to soften dark pencil lines
parallel lines that lie next to one another but never touch	**shade** make darker than the rest
sketch draw quickly and roughly	**vertical** line that is straight up and down

More Books to Read

Books About Drawing

Lacey, Sue. *People*. Brookfield, Connecticut: Copper Beech Books, 1999.

Maze, Stephanie. *I Want to Be a Fashion Designer*. San Diego: Harcourt Brace, 1999.

Books About Fashion

Hatt, Christine. *Clothes of the Modern World*. Columbus, Ohio: Peter Bedrick Books, 2002.

Wallner, Rosemary. *Fashion Designer*. Mankato, Minnesota: Capstone Books, 2001.

Watson, Linda. *Fashions: 1950–2000*. Pennsylvania: Chelsea House Publishers, 2000.

Index